How to Make Simple, Sturdy, Inexpensive Furniture from Cardboard

· ·

George deLucenay Leon

STACKPOLE
BOOKS

Published by
STACKPOLE BOOKS
5067 Ritter Road
Mechanicsburg, PA 17055

Printed in the United States of America

10 9 8 7 6 5 4 3 2 1

First Edition

Cover design by Caroline Miller
Photographs by George deLucenay Leon
Illustrations by Vantage Art, Inc.

Library of Congress Cataloging-in-Publication Data
Leon, George deLucenay.
    How to make simple, sturdy, inexpensive furniture from cardboard/
George deLucenay Leon. — 1st ed.
        p.   cm.
    ISBN 0-8117-2548-0
    1. Paper work. 2. Paperboard. 3. Furniture making. I. Title.
TT870.L446   1994
684.1'06—dc20   94-1632
                                                            CIP

To my wife, Stish, whose valuable input
as an interior designer is warmly appreciated

Contents

Acknowledgments

M y thanks to Arthur K. Meltzer, president of Keystone Paper, and to Arthur Merahn of the same company for taking time during their busy schedules to teach me what I know about cardboard. Any errors are my own.

My thanks also to the Reader's Digest Association for the use of material which previously appeared in "Practical Problem Solver," copyright © 1991. Used by permission.

Introduction

W hy build furniture out of corrugated cardboard? There are lots of good reasons. First, cardboard furniture is inexpensive. If you're trying to live within a small budget, you can furnish your apartment at relatively little cost. You may also want to build cardboard furniture as a model for another piece of furniture you're thinking of making or buying. You can build the piece to size and try it out in place for a while before you make a larger investment. Building out of cardboard allows you to try different types and pieces nearly for free. Your only cost is a little work. The biggest expense for the construction of the projects in this book was the adhesive—less than three dollars' worth for all the pieces I made!

Another reason is that cardboard furniture is perfect for children. You can make a quantity of scaled-down furniture that is ideal for a youngster. When the child grows out of it, the furniture can be discarded without the sense of wasted money. And, a child can carry cardboard furniture around without any danger to the youngster should it tip over.

Another advantage of cardboard is that it is available everywhere—and for free! Refrigerators, stoves, and other large objects are shipped in corrugated cardboard. You will find boxes of all shapes and sizes being thrown away. Stores are glad to get rid of what they otherwise would pay to have hauled away. A supermarket is an ideal source for practically every size and weight of corrugated cardboard you might need.

Cardboard furniture is also good for the environment. No trees are cut down to make your cardboard furniture (except what would have been cut anyway to make the cardboard). And you are recycling what would ordinarily end up in a landfill or an incinerator.

Corrugated cardboard has incredible strength for its weight. You can handle it easily, and you need only a sharp knife to cut it. No woodworking knowledge, no power tools, and no particular skills are required. Mistakes cost virtually nothing. All you have to do to remedy an error is cut another piece of cardboard. You can experiment to your heart's delight. Who knows what you could end up with?

Of course, you can't make a bed frame or a sofa from corrugated cardboard. But you can fashion a variety of tables, shelves, chests, etc. The projects in this book are only the tip of the iceberg. The only limit is your imagination.

Terms, Tools, and Tips

B efore you begin any of the projects in this book, it's a good idea to familiarize yourself with some of the very simple materials and processes you will use. Understanding the basics of cardboard construction will go a long way toward making your first projects successful.

Let's first define a few of the terms you're going to encounter as you go through the projects.

The words *panel* and *sheet* are used interchangeably.

Cardboard always means corrugated fiberboard. It comes in a variety of construction arrangements, thicknesses, and tensile strengths. The cardboard you need consists of sheets of heavy brown paper separated by one or more layers of fluted (corrugated) paper. The flat and corrugated sheets are glued together in such a way that they resemble a sandwich in which the corrugated sheets are the filling. Considering its weight and thickness, corrugated cardboard has remarkable strength.

When you are searching for cardboard for a specific project, you won't be able to specify the thickness or type; you have to take what you can find. But if you can recognize the various construction arrangements, you'll be able to tell if a particular piece has the strength needed for your intended project.

There are two types of corrugated cardboard you are likely to find: double faced sheets and double-wall sheets.

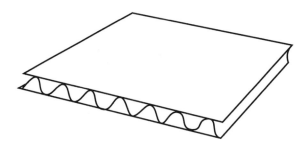

Double-faced sheets are a sandwich of two flat sheets glued to each side of the corrugated member. Most containers obtained from grocery or hardware stores are of this type, and you will probably be working with it most often.

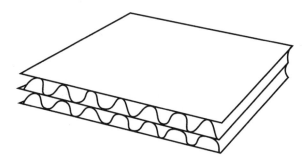

Double-wall sheets have a greater tensile strength than double-faced sheets. A double-wall sheet consists of three flat liners alternating with two corrugated members. This club-sandwich arrangement—flat liner, corrugated member, center flat liner, corrugated member, flat liner—produces a type of cardboard that is utilized for shipping objects that are heavy or fragile.

For our purposes, the double-wall variety is most useful for furniture that requires a great amount of strength. When it's not available, however, there is a perfectly acceptable substitute: Take sheets of the *double-faced* type of board and glue them face-to-face. By gluing two or even three sheets together, you obtain a panel which has extraordinary tensile strength.

Double-faced cardboard is almost $1/8$-inch thick. Although only one thickness may be listed for a project, a tabletop for example will require two or three thicknesses to achieve the necessary strength. See Tip 6. This means that measurements shown in the drawings are for the sake of the proportions. Your final thickness may differ, depending on the type of corrugated cardboard you employ, as well as the number of layers. The descriptions and drawings of the projects will explain where extra layers should be used to achieve the desired strength.

When you glue two or more sheets, place each sheet so that the corrugations are at right angles to adjacent sheets. This helps to prevent bending and adds strength.

For our use, *glue* refers to any adhesive such as a paper or library paste. To construct these projects, I recommend a commercial white paper paste, such as Elmer's Glue-All. Do not use water-based glues. The liquid can seep through, making the corrugations soggy. When this happens, the cardboard will lose its strength and be virtually useless. Don't use any of the fast-setting types of adhesives, either. When you glue sheets of cardboard together, you need some time to square the edges before the adhesive sets. That's why I recommend the type I do. It takes 15 to 20 minutes to set—ample time to adjust the sheets of cardboard exactly the way you want them.

You need only a few very basic tools to complete these projects:

• A utility knife with 2-inch changeable blades. The blade should always be razor-sharp. It can be sharpened on a fine oil stone or replaced.

• An X-acto knife with a pointed blade. This type of knife uses a blade no thicker than a razor blade. The blade is disposable and cannot be sharpened, so you should have several on hand.

• A 36-inch metal straightedge.

• A 12-inch plastic or metal triangle with 45- and 90-degree angles.

• A sanding block with medium or fine sandpaper. The block shown in the photo is 9 inches by 3 inches by 1 inch. A long block sands a straight edge better. Use one that fits your hand comfortably.

• Paper clamps to hold cardboard pieces in place while the glue sets. Have on hand half-a-dozen that are at least 2 to 3 inches long.

• Commercial white paper paste, such as Elmer's Glue-All, that sets in about 15 minutes.

• A roll of 2-inch-wide, self-sealing, cloth tape. Use it for binding edges together and for door hinges.

• Paint and shellac brushes.

• Contact paper, paint, and decals, as desired.

Over the years I've discovered a number of tips that

make working with cardboard much easier. If you read and follow these tips, you'll save yourself from having to learn the hard way.

TIP 1

Always use a very sharp knife. It's impossible to do good work without the proper tools, and a sharp knife is the most important. If you use a knife with a changeable blade, such as an X-acto knife, you can put a sharp blade in whenever you need one.

One further word about knives: Contrary to intuition, a sharp blade is less dangerous than a dull one. Cutting with a sharp blade requires less effort, and therefore there is less chance that the knife will slip. Although some of the projects in this book may be used by children, the work of cutting must be done by an adult.

TIP 2

An X-acto knife is better for cutting a curve than the bigger utility knife. The sharp pointed edge will result in a more even curve.

TIP 3

When you begin a cut, use the thinner blade to score lightly the surface of the cardboard. Follow with the utility knife to complete the cut.

TIP 4

Use a metal edge when making a straight cut. A plastic edge can get sliced into, making it useless for future work.

TIP 5

To do a perfect job of bending cardboard, follow these directions: On the side that is to be bent down, draw a line where the cardboard is to be bent. Place the metal straightedge along the line and lightly pierce the cardboard with the point of the X-acto blade. Don't go through to the other side. Do this about every ⅛ inch. Place the straightedge on the pierced line and hold it down tightly as you bend the cardboard over the edge of a table. With a little practice you'll get a perfectly straight bend each time.

TIP 6

The dimensions given for the projects in this book are not engraved in stone. They merely indicate the general proportions. Much depends on the size and thickness of the cartons you have at hand. If you make a radical change in one dimension, however, make a rough sketch of the project so you can see if other dimensions need to be changed as well.

TIP 7

For your first attempt at building cardboard furniture, pick a simple project. The book begins with the simplest projects, and they become more demanding as you progress. None require any previous knowledge of construction, and success with an early project will give you the confidence to tackle more complicated ones.

TABLES

E very table, whether it's an antique made of rare woods and worth a king's ransom or an aluminum picnic table, has two essential characteristics: a flat surface and a support for that surface. The tabletop can be round, square, rectangular, or irregular. The support can consist of a single leg or as many as eight.

I've come up with designs for three different tables that can be made of cardboard. All are different, but all have the same two elements in common.

Project 1
Occasional Table

This occasional table with a circular top and uncomplicated legs is useful and will look good anywhere. But above all, it is extremely simple to construct.

CONSTRUCTION

For the top, use at least three double-faced sheets of cardboard at least 30 inches square. Suppose you can't locate cardboard sheets that big?

A solution is to butt two or three smaller sheets together to form a sheet of at least the desired size. Tape them edge to edge with a cloth self-sealing tape. This is the first layer. Make the second and third layers the same way.

To make the 30-inch-diameter circle, take a piece of string about 18 inches long. Make a slip knot at one end of the string and loop it around the head of a push pin stuck approximately in the center of one sheet of cardboard. The pin will be the center of the circle. Tie the other end of the string to a pencil. Adjust the length of the string so that you can draw a circle of the size you want.

As long as your circle is even, don't worry if it's not exactly 30 inches across. Cut the circle carefully with a sharp X-acto knife. Sand the edge of the circle so that it is smooth and round.

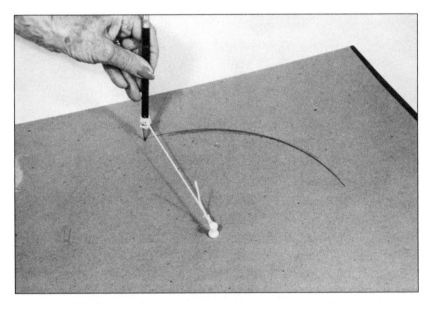

This first sheet is your pattern. Place it over as many sheets as you need for your table. Avoid having the joins on each sheet line up, and place each layer so that the corrugations are at right angles to the sheet(s) adjacent to it. This will give you added stiffness. Cut the circles out. Glue the layers together. Put weights over them and

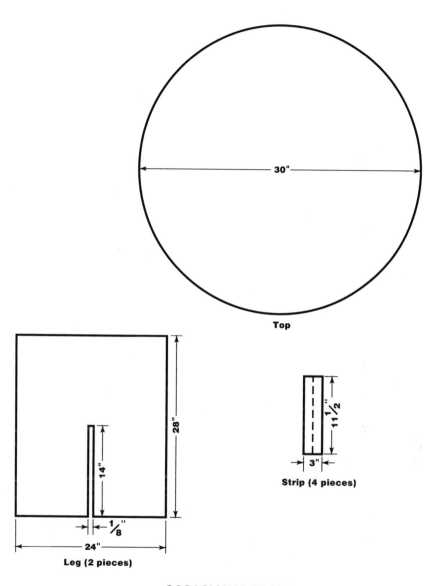

Top

Strip (4 pieces)

Leg (2 pieces)

OCCASIONAL TABLE

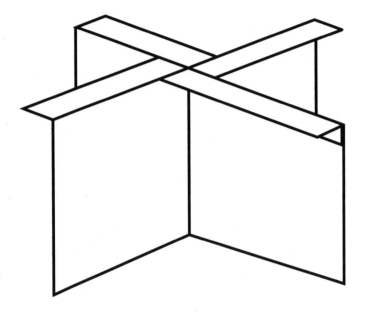

**OCCASIONAL TABLE
BASE**

allow them to dry. Then sand the edges until they are uniformly smooth.

While the tabletop dries, cut out the two pieces for the legs. Make two identical pieces approximately 24 inches wide by 28 inches high. You may vary the height if you wish, but make certain that the two pieces are exactly alike. If you don't think your cardboard is sufficiently sturdy, cut out two more panels with the same dimensions and glue them to the first two. Dry them under weights.

Cut a slit that has a **width equal to the thickness of the panel or panels.** The slit should be equal in length to half the height of the panel—14 inches as shown in the drawing. Slip the panels together. They should interlock to make a tight fit.

Cut four strips, 11½ inches by 3 inches, from scrap cardboard. Bend each in half along its length. Glue each one to the top of a leg. These strips are also to be glued to the underside of the tabletop. Turn the table upside down, apply the glue, and put under weights until the strips are dry. The basic construction is completed.

FINISHING

Use a throw that drapes down to the floor. Or, if you don't want to cover the table with a drape, you can apply gummed paper with a simulated wood grain. Add matching strips of gummed paper to cover the edges. If you want to protect your table against damp objects, give it a couple of coats of shellac instead of using the gummed paper.

No one will guess that this handsome table cost so little to make and was so easy to build. It serves as well as a store-bought unit, and it fits just as if you had a decorator make it to order. You also have the satisfaction of knowing that you did your bit in the recycling effort.

Variations: Change the size of the top. Substitute a square or rectangular top.

Child's version: Scaled down, this table is ideal for a

youngster. All you have to do is change the height to suit the size of the child. You might make the upright panels about 20 inches high and 14 inches wide. The diameter of the top should then be reduced to 20 inches. Reduce the length of the reinforcement strips to match the legs. Decorate the top with brightly colored paper or with a plain color the child can scrawl on with crayons.

Project 2
Parsons Table

A heavy cardboard box I found gave me an idea for a good, sturdy table for a child. It is based on the design for a Parsons table (so-named because it was developed by the Parsons School of Design). You may not find an identical box, but a box with similar dimensions will do just as well.

My particular box happened to measure 18 inches square and was 28 inches deep. The box you choose should have its opening on the long side. If you lay out the project with care, you can eliminate the side with the opening completely.

Your first step should be to decide on the size of the finished project. You don't have to follow the exact dimensions of your box. Improvisation is very much the name of the game with cardboard construction.

In my case, I changed only the height, deciding that legs 15 inches long would be about right. To be sturdy, the legs should not be less than 2 inches wide. To make the table resemble the original Parsons design, allow a return—that's the piece that goes all around just under the top—of two inches.

CONSTRUCTION

Using the ruler, mark off the legs and the return; these are indicated in the drawing by dotted lines. With a sharp X-acto knife and a steel guide to keep the knife from slipping, make the first cut along the dotted lines. Follow the indentations with the utility knife.

When the excess cardboard has been removed, buff the edges with the sanding block until you have a smooth finish.

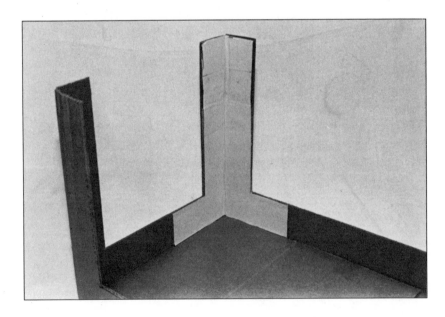

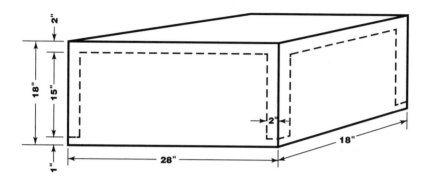

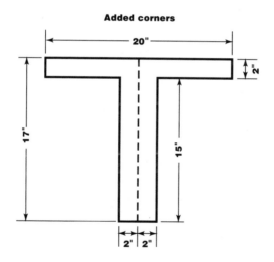

Added corners

PARSONS TABLE

If your box is not made of double-wall corrugated cardboard, you will need to add some reinforcements. To do that, cut out four T-strips of cardboard for the corners. The exact dimensions will depend on the actual height and width of the legs you made. Bend the cardboard—do not cut it—along the dotted line.

Push the T-shaped reinforcements into the corners from the inside, but don't glue them yet. When each is firmly in place, you will see that the edges are slightly wider than the table legs. This is to be expected. Trim each reinforcement so that it fits its leg perfectly. Now glue the reinforcements into the corners. Hold them in place with clamps until they are dry.

The use of reinforcements not only strengthens the legs, the extensions glued to the return furnish added support.

If your tabletop needs reinforcement, cut a rectangular piece of cardboard to match the top. Glue it in place and let it dry under weights.

FINISHING

I left my table unadorned for the photo, but you might paint your table or use contact paper with a wood finish. If you use contact paper, make sure you get enough to cut strips with which to cover the raw edges.

There are no sharp edges and no weight that could hurt a child. A youngster with youthful imagination can turn the table over and it becomes a boat or a train. Even the Concorde. Why not?

Project 3
Pedestal Table

The pedestal table doesn't need much floor space, and it can provide a multitude of services. It is made of only three rectangular parts: a top, a column, and a base.

Ideally, the top should be made of three sheets of double-wall cardboard. If you can't find that type, use four or even five sheets of double-faced board. The top must be solid enough to support some weight without sagging. The measurement shown is ½ inch, but you can make it thicker if it seems necessary. Feel free to vary the measurements to suit your needs; that's one of the advantages of making your own cardboard furniture.

CONSTRUCTION

Cut one panel for the top. Sand it and use it as a pattern for the others. Apply a generous amount of glue and stack the panels so the corrugations are at right angles to the adjacent layers. Place weights on them and let them dry thoroughly. Sand the edges smooth.

The pedestal, or column, is made from one piece of cardboard. In the pictured table, the piece measured 26 inches by 32 inches, but you may make a column of a different size. The corrugations should run vertically to accommodate the bending. In this case the solid lines indicate where the cuts are to be made; the dotted lines show where to make the bends.

Bend the pieces lengthwise as shown by the vertical dotted lines. Do this carefully so that your column is straight. Now bend flaps C, D, E, and F on the horizontal dotted lines. These flaps will be glued to the base. Flaps G, H, I, and J will be attached to the top.

Glue flap A to the inside of flap B. Your rectangular column should measure 5 inches by 8 inches by 25 inches if you are following the measurements in the drawing. Let it dry completely.

For the base, begin by cutting a piece of board 15 inches by 19 inches. Cut out the rectangular opening. Push the column through the opening, and make any adjustments necessary to get a snug fit.

Remove the column and cut at least two more pieces using the first as a pattern. Don't forget to allow for the thickness of the cardboard. These pieces will become the reinforcements inside the column. They must be trimmed so that they fit snugly against the original. The flaps marked C, D, E, and F are folded back against the underside of the base and glued in position. Now add layers of cardboard so that you have a base at least 3 inch-

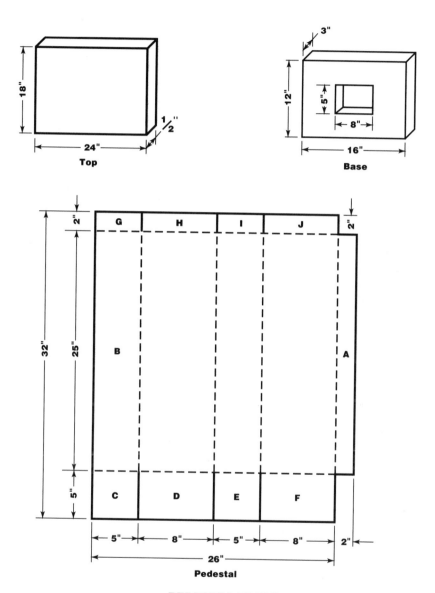

Top

Base

PEDESTAL TABLE

Pedestal

es thick. Use strips of board to fasten the corners in the inside. Glue them together. Once they are dry, push the column through the opening.

The final step is to glue the upper set of flaps (G, H, I, and J) to the underside of the top. Trim and sand the edges.

FINISHING

Finish with a coat of paint or cover with contact paper.

ACCESSORIES

The next six projects are items that can make your rooms a little more organized and your life a little easier. You can always use another wastebasket, magazine rack, or footstool. Place the octagonal stand in a number of rooms as an accent piece. Bulletin boards and boxes can bring order to your kitchen, family room, or bedrooms.

Project 4
Octagonal Stand

This octagon makes an ideal base on which to place a plant. You can make it in any size; the dimensions given below will help you with proportions.

CONSTRUCTION

Draw a circle 12 inches in diameter using the string-and-pencil technique shown for the occasional table. The circle can be drawn on paper or directly on cardboard. Through the center point draw a horizontal line to the edges of the circle marked A and E. Place your triangle

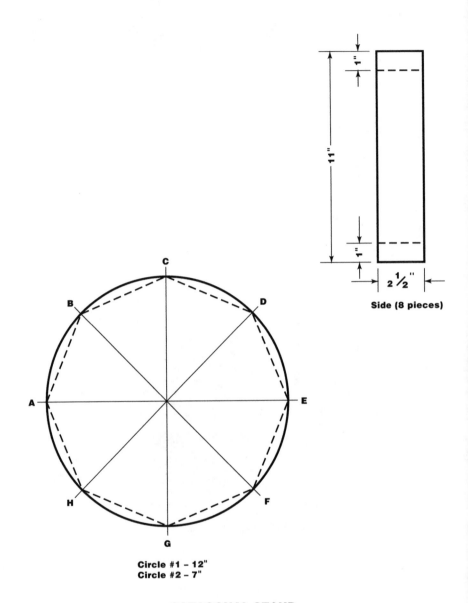

Side (8 pieces)

Circle #1 – 12"
Circle #2 – 7"

OCTAGONAL STAND

through the center and draw a vertical line intersecting the circle at points C and G. You have now divided the circle into four *equal* parts. Divide each of the four parts with the triangle by drawing lines through the center as shown in the drawing. The lines are B-F and D-H. There's your octagon.

Draw lines connecting each point to its two neighbors to make the edges of the octagon. These are indicated by the dotted lines. Cut along the dotted lines. If the cardboard seems fragile, cut and glue one or two additional panels to increase the strength. Use the first panel as a pattern.

Draw a 7-inch circle and mark it off as you just did for the bigger circle. Make the cuts along the dotted line to turn your circle into an octagon.

To avoid having to cut reinforcement pieces, find some heavy cardboard, and from it cut eight strips, each about 2½ inches wide and 11 inches long. Bend the strips 1 inch from each end.

Before you go any further, lightly sand the edges of all the components until they're smooth. Now you are ready to assemble your octagonal table.

Spread a generous amount of adhesive on one of the bent ends of a strip, and clamp it to the edge of one of the eight sides of the smaller circle. Do this with each of the eight strips. Let them dry thoroughly.

Now glue the free ends of the strips to the larger circle. Once the glue is dry, test the stand for strength. If it needs more support, glue reinforcement strips to the outsides of the legs.

FINISHING

Paint or finish your table as you like. If you intend to use the table as a plant stand, pick a finish that will repel water.

Project 5
Box

W hy make a box? Several projects require boxes of specific sizes. But you can't always find one with the size and shape required. And too often, the box you have on hand is not strong enough for your purposes.

Boxes are also the building blocks for drawers and drawer enclosures. A drawer is merely a box without a top; the holder (the part the drawer slides in to and out of) is also a box, with a top but without a front or a back. Since drawers and drawer holders have to be sized exactly, making your own to the size you need is often the best way to go.

Custom-sized boxes provide a shortcut for numerous construction projects. Once you've made one, you'll realize how easy it is.

The explanation that follows makes it easy for you to create a box or drawer. No dimensions are given in the directions. You fill in the dimensions for length, height, and width to design a box to meet your needs. It's really quite simple.

CONSTRUCTION

The first question to ask yourself is, "How big a piece of cardboard do I need for the drawer I have in mind?" To find out, you'll have to redo the drawing, substituting your own dimensions.

The drawing shows a rectangle—the usual shape of a drawer. The width of your drawer is equal to B in the drawing, C equals the length, and A is the height. Although the width will sometimes be greater than the length, the same principles will apply.

Get a large piece of paper, one that is larger than the actual size of the drawer. In the center of your paper, draw the rectangle with the dimensions you have decided on. This is the section labeled *bottom*. The dotted lines show where you will bend the cardboard. Mark them the same way on your drawing.

There is a narrow slit, not more than $\frac{1}{8}$ inch, between A and B (see the drawing). This slit is made to allow the strips to bend more easily and to make the sides perfectly vertical. Little things like this will make your finished project look better.

Draw the outline. Check your dimensions several times to avoid any possible mistakes. Use carbon paper to copy your drawing onto the cardboard. If possible, lay the drawing on the panel so that the corrugations run the long way.

Make your cuts as shown by the solid lines. The dotted lines indicate where you bend the cardboard. The C flaps are bent up, and the A flaps are glued to the inside of the B flaps. Glue in place and let the whole thing dry.

Construction of the drawer holder: A drawer must be able to slide in and out of a piece of furniture. For this you need a custom drawer holder, which will be slightly larger than the drawer it will hold.

Make a drawing similar to the drawer illustration, but eliminate the A and B flaps. Add $\frac{1}{8}$ inch to $\frac{1}{4}$ inch to the height and width of the drawer. Fold on the dotted lines and glue the C flaps to the inside of the furniture piece.

That's all there is to it! There's no need to finish it because the holder will not show.

Box • 31

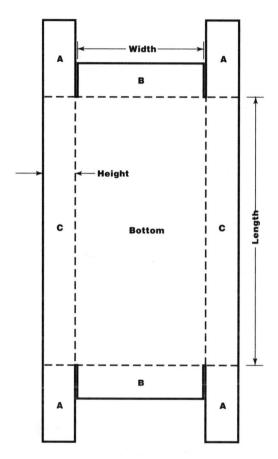

BOX-DRAWER

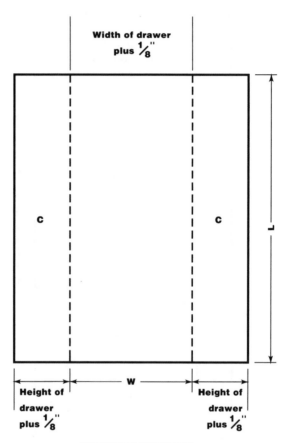

DRAWER HOLDER

Box • 33

FINISHING

A couple of coats of shellac will make the drawer more durable. You can use any type of pull you wish; simply pierce the cardboard as if it were wood. If it seems necessary, you can glue a piece of cardboard to the inside of the drawer to reinforce the area where the pull fits.

Project 6
Bulletin Board

Bulletin boards are ideal for tacking up telephone numbers, recipes, project steps, favorite cartoons, and dozens of other things. They are especially handy as message centers in busy households.

While I was working on this book, I realized I needed some visual means to keep track of where I was in the process of each project. What I needed was a large bulletin board, one larger than was commercially available.

CONSTRUCTION

I started with a piece of corrugated cardboard that measured 24 inches by 32 inches, but you can use any size that suits your needs. Most double-faced board is not thick enough to hold push pins, so you will want to spot-glue together two thicknesses. Put weights on the pieces and let them dry.

FINISHING

The bulletin board doesn't require any finishing, but if you're feeling creative, you might want to cover the board with an attractive fabric or paper. Glue or tack the covering in place, or fasten the covering to the back with wide tape.

Hang your bulletin board by tacking it to the wall or attach a wire and hang it from a single nail. Then all you need is a box of push pins to hold your reminders in place.

Who would guess that your board didn't come from an expensive stationer? And yet you made it yourself, at no cost and in less time than it would have taken to go out and buy one.

Project 7
Wastebasket

A wastebasket always comes in handy, and this one is easily made.

The project consists of only four pieces of corrugated cardboard, one piece for a base, and four reinforcement strips. An hour or two is all it takes to create a very useful piece of furniture.

As you probably know by now, you don't have to use the exact dimensions of the drawing. You must remember, however, that once you change one dimension, you will have to change others. Don't worry if you forget though. New pieces are free, and cutting them costs only a little time.

I made my wastebasket with a rounded top to give it a little flair, but you can have square, rounded, or wavy tops. Use your imagination and cut the tops in a pattern that pleases you.

CONSTRUCTION

If you want to make the rounded top, draw a line 12 inches long on a piece of paper. Mark one end of the line A and the other B, as shown in the drawing. Now, mark the center point and label it C. Set your drawing compass on C and extend it so that it reaches A and B. Draw a half circle.

Ten inches below the A-B line draw another line (D-E) 8 inches long. Its midpoint (F) should be exactly below point C. Draw a line from A to D and from B to E. You now have the pattern for one leaf or side of the wastebasket.

Use this pattern to cut out four leaves from some double-faced cardboard. If this doesn't seem to be sufficiently strong, cut out eight leaves and glue them in pairs. Use a sharp X-acto blade to cut the rounded (or patterned) tops. Sand all the edges lightly for a smooth finish.

Now cut the base. You want a square piece of cardboard measuring 10 inches on a side. Mark off 1 inch from each of the four edges. Cut the 1-inch squares out of each corner and bend the flaps along the dotted lines. The result is a square base 8 inches on a side.

Add paste to one of the bent flaps of the base. Glue the bottom of one leaf to that portion of the base, making sure you have the edges square. Clamp the pieces, and then connect the other three leaves to the base. Do not connect the leaves to each other until you are satisfied they are fastened securely to the base.

You will need additional support to connect the sides. Cut four strips measuring 9 inches by 2 inches by 2½ inches with lengthwise corrugations. Bend these strips along the dotted lines.

Each strip must be adjusted so that the bottom end is flush against the base and the leaves are held together tightly. Apply the glue and clamp the pieces. Repeat the procedure until all four strips are in place. Some care

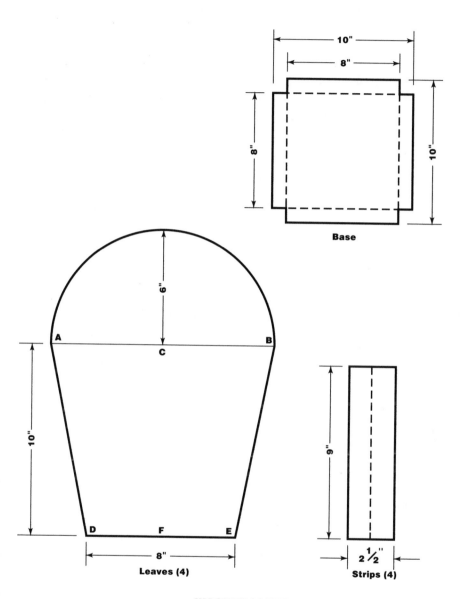

Base

6"

A   B
C

10"

D   F   E

8"

Leaves (4)

9"

2 1/2"

Strips (4)

WASTEBASKET

here will make your basket attractive and free of wobbles. Let all the pieces dry thoroughly.

FINISHING

A couple of coats of shellac will help preserve the surface of the cardboard and give it a glossy finish. You can also cover your wastebasket with patterned contact paper or paint it to match other furniture in the room.

Project 8
Magazine Rack

Every comfortable chair needs a rack next to it to hold magazines, the TV listings, knitting, or whatever you need to occupy yourself while you relax. This quickly and easily built magazine rack serves its purpose many times over. Making it is simple, and the project can be finished in less time than it takes to describe how to do it.

CONSTRUCTION

Using the illustration as a guide, cut out the required pieces. To make the end pieces, choose a piece of cardboard measuring at least 12 inches by 15 inches. Lightly mark a vertical line 15 inches long. This is line A-G on the drawing.

Mark a point on the line 10 inches from the bottom. This is point D. This point should be 5 inches below G.

At the bottom of line A-G, draw a horizontal line 5 inches long with point A in the center. This is line B-C in the drawing. Through point D draw a horizontal line 12 inches long with D at the center. This is line E-F. Through point G draw a horizontal line 7 inches long with G at the center. This is line H-I. Connect points B, E, and H with one line and points C, F, and I with another. With lines B-C and H-I, this completes the outline for the end pieces.

You need two such pieces. Cut one out and, after you sand the edges, use it as a pattern for the second. If the cardboard doesn't seem sturdy enough, add additional sheets.

Cut the two sides. The dotted lines show where the cardboard is bent to meet the end pieces. Then cut the base. The flaps, indicated by the dotted lines, are bent and glued to the ends and to the sides. Use clamps to hold the sides while they're setting.

While those pieces dry, cut the divider. The dotted lines show where to bend the flaps that are glued to the ends. Notice the unusual bending pattern; one flap is bent in the opposite direction of the other. Through this arrangement, the divider provides equal strength to both sides. When the other pieces are dry and the divider is cut, glue it to the ends. Remember to clamp the parts together until they are completely dry.

Next cut the cardboard for the four feet. Each foot is made of about six square pieces of board $3/4$ inch to 1 inch on a side. Cut all the pieces from the same sheet so that the four feet are of equal height. Glue six pieces face to face to make one foot, and do the same for each of the other feet. Dry them under weights. Then glue each foot to a corner of the rack. Be generous with the adhesive.

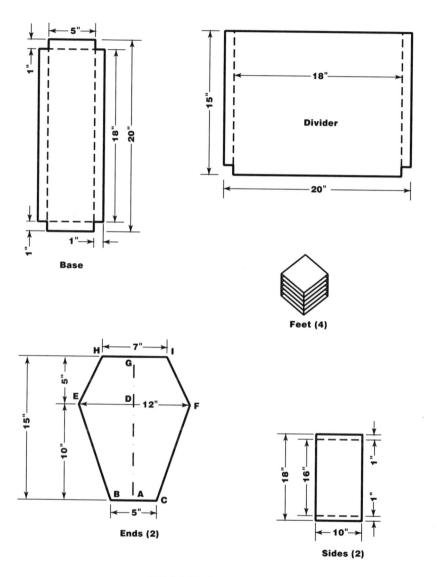

Base

Divider

Feet (4)

Ends (2)

Sides (2)

MAGAZINE RACK

FINISHING

A wood-grain contact paper is perfect to finish the project. Or you can paint it a color that matches your comfortable chair. No matter how you finish it, you will get a lot of satisfaction from this simple project.

Project 9
Footstool

A t the end of a long day, rest your weary feet on this handy piece of furniture. All you need to add for complete comfort is a throw pillow.

CONSTRUCTION

Cut out the parts as indicated on the drawing. The dimensions given suggest general proportions; they do not have to be followed exactly. Depending on the thickness of the cardboard you are using, you may need to adjust some of the dimensions.

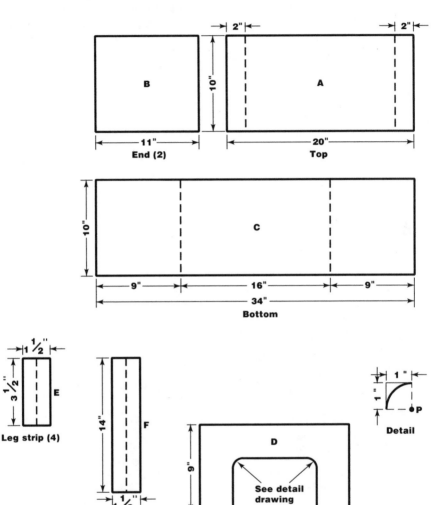

FOOTSTOOL

The side panels (D) are rounded to make the unit more attractive, but this is optional. If you want to duplicate the curve, follow the detailed drawing. Mark 1 inch from the corner both horizontally and vertically. Connect the lines from those points to point P. With a compass or the bottom of a small glass, draw a curve that touches the two points you just marked. Almost any curve will do as long as they are all alike. Cut on the lines you drew.

Draw panels A, B, C, and D and cut them out.

The flaps on part A are bent upward, and the flaps on part C are bent downward. Glue the middle section of C to the middle section of A. Once these pieces are dry, place one of the B panels so that its bottom edge is lined up with the bottom edge of C. This brings the top of panel B about 2 inches above C. Follow the same procedure for the other end of the unit.

The two side pieces (D) are attached to the sides of C by means of the side strips (F). Parts B are fastened to the side pieces by means of the leg strips (E). These strips also contribute to the strength of the legs.

The flaps of A are glued to the end pieces. Clamp them securely while they dry. Sand all the edges until they are smooth.

FINISHING

The footstool in the photograph was covered with a maroon paint. Wood-grain contact paper would also provide a handsome finish.

LARGE STORAGE PROJECTS

$\bullet$

The following projects came about as the result of a lucky accident. A gas heater had been delivered to one of my neighbors, and I found the carton it came in lying on the sidewalk. The heavy corrugated cardboard carton was in excellent condition—only the top was missing. Seeing the box lying there gave me several ideas for projects, among them the wardrobe, closet, and blanket chest that are described in the following pages. See what you can come up with when you use your imagination.

This particular carton measured 62 inches high, 24 inches wide, and 19 inches deep. Refrigerators, stoves, and some heating units are packed in cartons not too dissimilar. These cartons will likely not have the same measurements as mine, but they'll do fine for the job. The corrugated cardboard is usually strong and suitable for a variety of projects.

Finishing: Regardless of the use to which you put your carton, you should paint it with a couple of coats of shellac or a coat of water-based paint, or you could cover it with contact paper, if you prefer.

Project 10
Wardrobe

My large carton seemed perfect for making a wardrobe closet. It had been manufactured by overlapping a narrow piece of one side to another by a couple of inches. This suggested using the existing overlap as a hinge for the door—there was no need to fabricate one. The major modifications I needed to make to my carton were to add a top and a base. Then I added the clothes rod.

CONSTRUCTION

If your box resembles mine, you need to cut the front panel along the unhinged side and across the top and bottom. This allows the door to swing on its hinge.

If you need a top, glue two layers of cardboard together, and glue them to the walls by means of an overlap, as you've done with earlier projects.

Constructing a base for your closet will allow the door to open without scraping along the floor. The base is to be glued to the finished container, so it is important for the finished base to have the same dimensions as those of the bottom of the basic unit.

On the drawing, the dotted lines on the base show where the cardboard is to be bent down. The solid lines indicate where cuts are to be made. This results in a base 2 inches high after the sides of the base are glued at each corner. Strengthen the sides of the base with an extra thickness of cardboard.

Next, cut the cardboard strips for along the door. These strengthen the door frame and provide a decorative border to cover the raw edges. The strips are 2 inches wide and butted end to end. Use plenty of glue to fasten them in position. Add panels of corrugated cardboard to the inside of the door for additional strength and to eliminate wobble. Always use added panels on large projects.

You now need to add holders for the clothes rod. Bend a scrap piece of cardboard into a half circle. The piece should be deep enough to provide adequate support for the rod. Glue one edge of the half circle to a 4-inch-

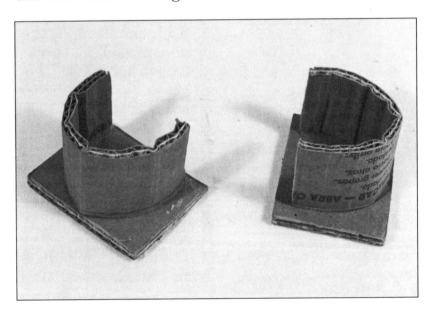

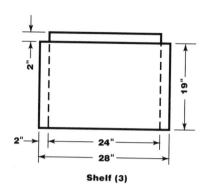

Shelf (3)

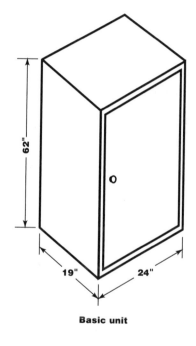

Basic unit

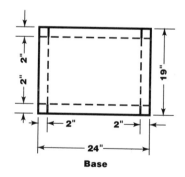

Base

WARDROBE

square piece of cardboard. Make a second holder the same way. Glue the holders into the sides of the wardrobe at the desired height and about halfway between the front and the back.

The clothes rod can be made of any cylinder of wood, plastic, or cardboard. Cut the rod so that it is just long enough to fit snugly into the holders.

FINISHING

Put a decorative knob on the front of the door and another on the side next to the opening. A cord looped around both knobs will keep the door closed. Your finished wardrobe is ideal for hanging clothes that belong to another season.

Project 11
Storage Closet

Another use for your large appliance box is to make a storage closet from it. That's simple. You simply make the door and the base as described for the wardrobe, but instead of installing holders and a rod, you put in shelves. Put only one shelf in, near the top, if you're going to store mops and brooms. Or, for linen storage, install several shelves. You can make as many shelves as you want.

CONSTRUCTION

The size of the shelves will be dependent on the size of the carton you're working with. The shelves should reach all the way to the back of the closet. Use double thicknesses of cardboard for the shelves, more if you want to store heavier items.

Turn down a 2-inch strip at each side and along the back of each shelf. Glue the flaps to the closet walls and back. This will provide a strong support for the shelf. Space the shelves according to the items you want to store in your closet.

Project 12
Blanket Chest

D on't need a closet? How about a blanket chest? Lay the carton on its back and . . . voila! You have a blanket chest!

CONSTRUCTION

Cut the door as explained for the wardrobe. It's up to you as to whether to reinforce the door, but the sides and back are fine as is. Add moth balls, and your blankets will be as safe as if they were in a cedar chest.

FURNITURE FOR EVERY ROOM

Y ou'll be surprised at how many different places you'll find to use the remaining projects.

You may also be surprised at how sturdy these items can be. Properly constructed, this shelving, nightstand, chest, hutch, and desk can support the weight required of them.

You can paint them or cover them with contact paper to match or accent the other pieces of furniture in the room.

Project 13
Corner Shelving

This four-shelved corner unit is bound to come in handy to fill a vacant corner. And it's easy to construct. All you need are two identical boxes. I put mine together using two strong egg storage boxes I got from a local grocery store. My boxes measured 12 inches square and were almost 14 inches high. Of course, your boxes are likely to have different measurements. That really doesn't matter, just so the two boxes are identical.

CONSTRUCTION

Start with one box and glue the covers together so they form a stable upper and lower closure. Now, looking down on the top of your box, draw a diagonal from one corner to the other, as shown in the drawing. The dotted lines A-E, E-D, B-D, and B-A show where to cut to form two triangular sections. Cut similar diagonals along the other end of the box. These cuts will divide the box into two equal end parts. Cut the second box the same way.

Your boxes need not be exactly the same as those in the drawing. As long as your boxes are alike, your shelves' variances are not important. Study the drawings carefully before you make the cuts. What is important is that the four shelves be identical.

The leftover cardboard may be used to make the triangular panels that are fitted between each shelf. Each panel is glued to the shelf above and beneath it. You will also need two additional panels to glue to the vertical sides of the assembled shelves. They help hold the shelving together and add stability.

Now make the base. You will have to adjust the measurements to suit your boxes. Refer to the drawing to see

where to cut (the solid lines) and where to bend (the dotted lines). The end pieces are glued to the strips to solidify the base. Clamp them together while they are drying. Glue each shelf to the one beneath it. Dry under weights.

Now add 1-inch edge strips to the sides and bottom edges of the shelving. This edging hides the raw edges of the cardboard, gives strength to the unit, and frames each shelf attractively. Before you glue them in place, sand the edges of the strips so they are smooth. The

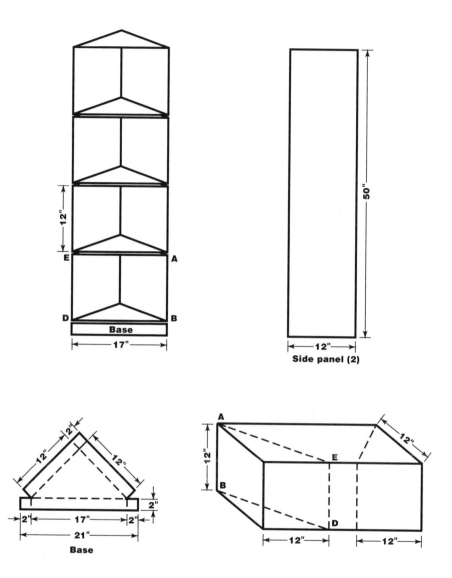

Side panel (2)

Base

CORNER SHELVING

easiest way to join the strips is to butt them together at right angles. If you're willing to take the time, however, mitering them at a 45-degree angle will give the finished project a handsome look. The horizontal strip at the bottom of each shelf is glued to the shelf beneath it.

FINISHING

Once all the glue is dry, your shelves are ready to be painted. Stand the shelving in a corner, and fill it with your favorite collectibles.

Project 14
Nightstand

Everyone needs a little table next to the bed to hold a lamp, telephone, glasses, reading material, and whatever else you want near you while you're in bed. This unit has a drawer and a shelf to make it even more handy. But don't let its detailed appearance fool you; constructing this piece is a straightforward job.

As usual, the size of your nightstand depends on your needs and the materials you have at hand. The stand should be about 6 inches higher than the bed for maximum usefulness. Try to find some double-wall cardboard, at least for the supporting sides. If you can't find the heavier grade, then use two or even three thicknesses of the double-faced board to compensate.

CONSTRUCTION

First cut out the top, bottom, and sides of the stand. If you're following the pattern, you will need two side panels (24 inches by 16 inches), two panels for top and bottom (14 inches by 16 inches), and the back (14 inches by 24 inches). Cut all of these pieces out.

Glue the sides and back together so that the top and bottom panels fit inside the walls. Use reinforcement strips in the corners along connecting panels. If you need additional stability, glue more panels where it seems necessary.

Now cut a piece of cardboard 30 inches by 16 inches to serve as the bottom shelf. Bend along the dotted lines as indicated in the drawing. If you can't find a panel that large, make the shelf out of a panel measuring 14 inches by 16 inches. Then use two edge panels (8 inches by 16 inches) to support the shelf. You'll have to use two strips (4 inches wide and 16 inches long) for support. Bend them lengthwise down the middle and glue them to the side panels and the shelf.

The finished drawer shown in the photograph is $13\frac{1}{2}$ inches wide, 3 inches high, and 15 inches deep. You can make it from one piece of cardboard $13\frac{1}{2}$ inches wide and 21 inches long. Lay out and mark the piece as shown in the drawing. The tiny slits—not more than $\frac{1}{8}$ of an inch—result in a better drawer. Without them, the cardboard will not make a smooth bend. The slits are important in creating drawers with good vertical sides. Remember that the drawer should be almost $\frac{1}{4}$ inch narrower than the channel it moves in.

The false front panel keeps the drawer from being pushed too far in. Its measurements are slightly larger than those of the drawer. The $\frac{1}{2}$-inch strips should be placed at the very edges of the false front panel. You can miter or butt the corners of the edge strips. Mitering looks much nicer than butting, but it requires a little more effort.

The drawer holder can be made with one panel measuring 16 inches by 18 inches. Bend 2-inch flaps on each of the ends, and glue the flaps to the sides.

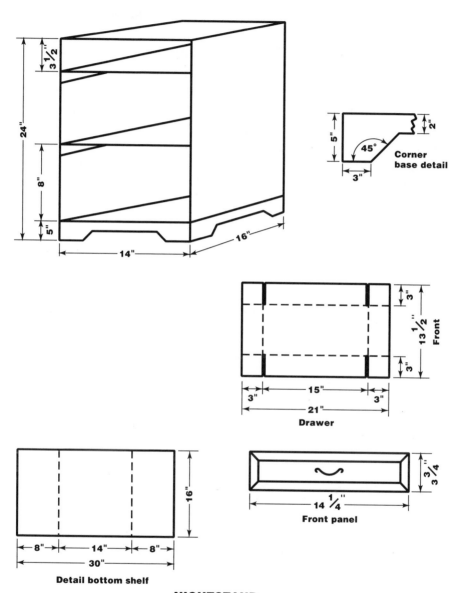

Corner
base detail

Drawer

Front panel

Detail bottom shelf

NIGHTSTAND

Now it's time to construct the base. Remember that you want the tabletop about 6 inches higher than the bed. Figure out how high to make the base by subtracting the height of the unit without the base from the desired height. For a 5-inch base, you need four pieces 6 inches high, two that are 14 inches long and two that are 16 inches long. They can be left solid or cut out as shown in the detail. The angled corners are a nice touch.

To be sure that your nightstand can hold the lamp and books you'll put on it, it needs to be sturdy. You may want to add another layer of cardboard to each of the base pieces before you assemble it. Join the four sides of the base using reinforcement strips.

Turn the unit upside down and glue the base to the bottom of the stand. Let everything dry thoroughly, and then sand all the pieces.

FINISHING

Put the final touches on your nightstand by covering it with contact paper. Or paint it to match the bedroom color scheme.

Project 15
Bookshelf

This easily built bookshelf is a handy piece of furniture. It can be used as a stand-alone unit, or combined with the chest to make a hutch.

CONSTRUCTION

Begin with the exterior of the unit. Cut the two side panels (8 inches by 32 inches). Then cut the back panel (32 inches by 34 inches). Feel free to change these dimensions to suit your needs or the corrugated cardboard available.

Glue the back to the sides by means of the two strips that bend forward. These should be glued to the outside of the side panels. Allow this assembly to dry under weights.

Now cut four identical pieces 11 inches by 38 inches. One is the top, one the bottom, and the other two are the interior shelves. Using the dotted lines as guides, bend the flaps at each end. Pierce the dotted lines with the point of an X-acto blade to get good sharp bends.

Glue the top shelf to the sides and the back by means of the bent-down flaps. Check to make sure you have a right angle between all the pieces before you go any further.

Turn the unit upside down and glue the bottom to the sides and the back. The flaps should be glued to the inside of the panels. Use the adhesive generously to fix the sides and back solidly in place.

Once the glue is dry and the unit seems sturdy, the next step is to add the two center shelves. Along the inside of the sides, measure and mark 10 inches from the top and 10 inches from the bottom. This is where you will put the shelves. Bend the shelves' flaps up and glue them to the sides and the back. Before clamping them, check that the shelves are absolutely level. You'll have to do this quickly before the glue sets.

Cut out three more panels the same size as the finished shelves. These should not have flaps. Simply lay one on top of each middle shelf and the base and glue it in position. This will provide extra strength for the shelves.

Now cut two pieces 6 inches by 30 inches for the sides. These are to be butted against the flaps from the back panel that are glued to the outside of the sides. These added panels disguise the flaps coming from the back panel and make the sides smooth. Glue these panels in place. You may want to add a third layer on each side. These pieces would be 8 inches by 30 inches.

Cut strips of cardboard 1 inch wide to cover the raw

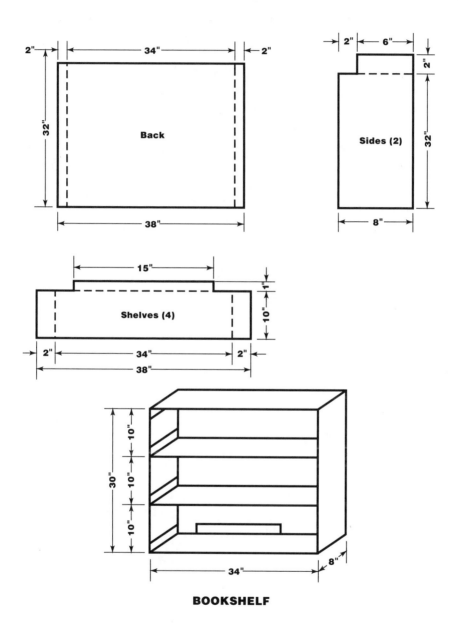

BOOKSHELF

edges. Use these strips as facing for the front of the shelves, as well as for the sides. They add a professional look to your bookshelf. If you don't want to cut the strips, you can cover the edges with cloth tape.

FINISHING

Paint or varnish your bookshelf. Using a contrasting color on the facing strips is an especially decorative touch.

One note of caution: Do not fill the shelves with too many heavy books. Even double layers of corrugated cardboard will bend eventually if they are overloaded. Put lightweight objects in the center and put your books on the ends.

Project 16

....

Chest

T his piece of furniture can serve several functions. As shown in the photograph, it's a mock dry sink used for storage. With a bookshelf set on top, it's a hutch. You can probably think of many ways to put such a piece to use.

The chest is quite simple to build; basically it's a box with a door. If you have a box of appropriate dimensions, it is almost no work at all. If, however, you intend to stack the bookshelf on top of the chest, it's important that the chest be the same width or a little wider. If no box is readily available, then you need to construct your own. Use double-wall cardboard or make sheets of two, preferably three, panels of double-faced corrugated cardboard.

CONSTRUCTION

If you're starting from scratch, cut two panels 34 inches by 32 inches for the front and back of the chest. If you need double- or triple-thick panels, make sure the corrugations run perpendicular on adjacent sheets. Also cut two side panels 16 inches by 32 inches.

The top and bottom panels should each measure 16 inches by 34 inches. The panels will be joined together by means of supporting strips 2 inches wide and as long as the length of the panels to which they will attach. These strips will be bent in the middle to form a right angle and used as reinforcements where the side panels meet the front and back.

Assemble the top, bottom, and side panels; the front panel will come later. Glue them together using reinforcement strips for each corner. You should now have a strong box capable of sustaining its own contents plus the weight of the bookshelf, if you decide to combine the two.

Now you're ready to finish off the front panel. Cut the opening for the door before you add the panel to the unit. The opening should measure about 11 inches wide and 19 inches high. The door panel should be about 1/4 inch less on each side—just enough so that the door can open without obstruction.

Cut the 2-inch strips to hang vertically on either side of the door, as well as the 6-inch strips that go across the top and the bottom of the front of the chest. Their primary purpose is decorative, but they do make the front of the chest stronger.

Sand the edges of the opening and the edges of the door to prevent snagging. The 1-inch edging strips on the top, bottom, and one side of the door should overlap the

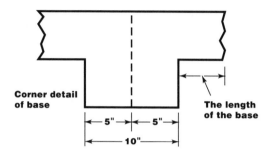

Corner detail
of base

The length
of the base

5" · 5"

10"

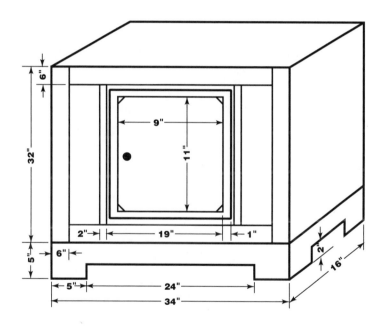

CHEST

door edges by ¼ inch to prevent it from being pushed through the opening. The hinge side does not require an overlap.

Measure and cut the strips, but don't glue them to the door yet; you have to make the hinges. Three pieces of heavy cloth tape, each about 3 inches long and 2 inches wide, will hold the door nicely. Place the hinges in position and then glue a 1-inch edging strip over them.

The base is similar to the one used for the wardrobe and should raise the unit 5 inches off the floor. Use at least two thicknesses of cardboard, more if you are going to build a hutch. Cut two strips 34 inches long and two strips 16 inches long. All four strips should be 6 inches wide. If you like, you can cut out the corners for a more decorative look, or leave the base solid.

Turn the chest upside down. Fit the base to the chest and make the necessary adjustments so that the base fits correctly. Glue the bent-over strips to the bottom of the chest. You may want to use reinforcement strips to secure the base to the bottom of the chest. This will insure that the base doesn't slip out from under the chest.

FINISHING

I finished my chest by painting it dark green and applying clear varnish to the facing strips for contrast. This gave it an antique look. Use your imagination to come up with a beautiful finish for your chest.

Project 17
Hutch

A hutch is a very useful piece of furniture in the dining room. You can store and display china on the open shelves and put linens and tableware in the enclosed chest beneath. You'll wonder how you ever got along without it.

CONSTRUCTION

Follow the directions for completing the bookshelf and the chest. Now, simply position the shelving on top of the chest and glue it in place. Use strips of cardboard or tacks pushed in along the open shelves to keep your dishes from slipping. What could be simpler?

Project 18
....
Writing Desk

This desk is perfect for writing letters, paying bills, and doing homework. And if you don't need it for any of those purposes, use it to add a decorative touch to any space. Finished with care, this functional desk can end up as the focus of your room.

The drawer sections for this piece are very similar to those of the nightstand. The basic construction is identical; only the dimensions vary.

The desk is made up of four independently constructed sections. Sections A and B are identical. Section C is the top of the desk, and section D forms a bridge between sections A and B.

CONSTRUCTION

Start with two identical boxes that are large enough to make two enclosures approximately 12 inches by 20 inches by 30 inches. Reinforce each panel by joining additional sheets firmly to the sides and the back.

Assemble the sides, back, top, and the shelves for sections A and B. (For a refresher on how to do the shelves, see the nightstand project.) The lowest shelf serves as the bottom of each section. Add at least one extra layer of cardboard to each shelf. This will add support and separate the drawers, preventing them from snagging as they are pulled.

Once assembled, glue the A section together and then the B section. While the adhesive sets, begin constructing the eight drawers. If you can find boxes of the appropriate size, use them as the basis for the drawers. Otherwise, construct them yourself, using the drawing as a guide. One piece of double-faced cardboard is sufficient for each drawer.

Try making one drawer and fitting it in the shelf before you build the others. It's best to find out now whether it's too tight or too loose. The drawers must be able to slide in and out without too much friction or wobble. If it doesn't fit, make adjustments until you get it right. When you have a drawer that fits well, use it as a pattern for the others. Remember, though, that the shelves themselves may vary, so make sure your drawer is custom-fit for its holder.

Next, construct the false fronts for the drawers. The front should be just a little larger than its drawer to keep the drawer from pushing through. This is accomplished by gluing 1-inch strips to the false front, leaving a slight overhang.

Now each section needs a base. They're built in the same way as bases for the other projects. You might

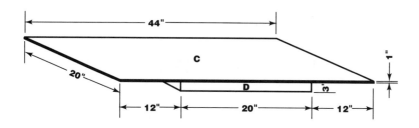

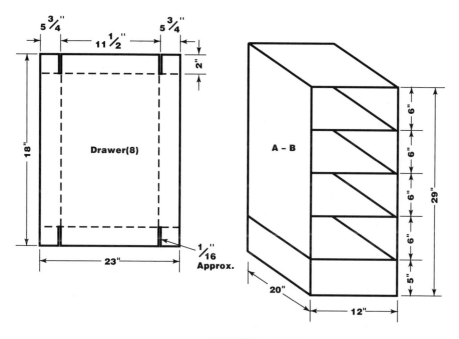

WRITING DESK

want to review the directions for the wardrobe. Six inches should be about right to bring the desk up to a comfortable height for writing, but you can size the bases to suit yourself. Each base consists of one set of two cardboard strips measuring 12 inches long and a second set measuring 20 inches long. The width of the strips is dependent on how high you want your desk. You'll want several thicknesses of cardboard to make sure that the base can support the weight of the desk as well as the force of someone working on it. Add reinforcement strips on the corners to hold the parts of the base together.

Section C is simply several 20-inch-by-44-inch panels glued together (with corrugations at right angles) to form a 1-inch-thick top for your desk. The top must be strong enough not to sag when someone leans on the desk to work.

You can make section D in one of three ways, depending on how much work you want to do. The quick-and-easy way is to cut one strip of cardboard 28 inches by 3 inches. Bend back 4 inches at each end of the strip. The bent portions will later be glued to the insides of sections A and B.

A second way is to do essentially the same thing, but make it a little nicer by adding a false drawer front. The false front is made by cutting an extra thickness of cardboard measuring 18 inches by 3 inches. Use strips the same width as for the real drawers to outline the false front. If you do a good job, no one will be able to tell it's not a real drawer.

The third possibility is to make a real drawer. This takes some additional work, but you have the convenience of an extra drawer for office supplies and other small items.

Make the drawer holder first. Its finished dimensions are 12 inches by 20 inches by 3 inches. The two 10-inch upper flaps must be glued to the underside of section C. Before you glue the holder in place, however, build the drawer to make sure it will fit. Its dimensions are shown in the drawing. Make all the necessary adjustments to the drawer and holder before you install the holder.

Now that you've got all the sections constructed, it's time to put the whole thing together. Lay section C over sections A and B. Bring A and B together so that they butt against the drawer holder. Glue the bent portions of section D to the inner sides of A and B.

FINISHING

The right choice of varnish or paint will leave you with a beautiful project that you can be proud of. The finished desk is as attractive and as functional as any wooden desk.

Child's version: Children often need a desk at which to play or do homework. Depending on the size of the child, you may need to resize the entire project. A simpler option, however, may be simply to eliminate the base and rest the desk directly on the floor.